Notes from a Eucharistic Life

Manon Ceridwen James

Leaf by Leaf is an imprint of Cinnamon Press.
www.cinnamonpress.com

ISBN 978-1-78864-984-1

British Library Cataloguing in Publication Data. A CIP record for this book can be obtained from the British Library.

Designed and typeset in Bodoni by Cinnamon Press. Cover design Adam Craig from original artwork:

© Christine Kinsey:

Ymson 1 / Soliloquy 1 (manyleb / detail) olew ar gynfas / oil on canvas 152.5 x 152.5 cm

Cinnamon Press is represented by Inpress Ltd.

Acknowledgements

I am very grateful to Jan Fortune for all her support in bringing this collection to birth, and in particularly to her and Cinnamon Press in giving me a part bursary towards their excellent Pencil mentoring scheme. I was very fortunate to be working with Helen May Williams and I am very grateful to her for her challenge, encouragement and insight. I also want to thank staff past and present at the Tŷ Newydd National Writing Centre for their excellent courses which were a real encouragement as I began to write poetry again. The poets who have helped me with some of the poems in this collection are: the late Nigel Jenkins, Sarah Kennedy, Kim Moore, John Fraser Williams, Zoe Skoulding, Gillian Clarke, Carol Ann Duffy, Jonathan Edwards. I am very grateful to them for their help, either as friends or as teachers on courses, or both! Christine Evans was my English teacher at school, and I am very grateful to her for that initial inspiration which continues to this day. Thanks too to Menna Elfyn who has generously allowed me to use her work in my own academic work, and for her continuing influence and inspiration.

I am also very grateful to my parishioners, students and colleagues for their support past and present and for the fun and friendship. Finally, my heartfelt thanks go to my Mam and Dad, my daughters, Miriam and Catrin and my step son Harri for their love and to Dylan to whom I dedicate this collection.

Some of the poems have been previously published, with thanks to the editors:
'Another Salem', 'Travelling by Train', 'Theology Seminar', 'A priest at a funeral' have been published in *Envoi* Issue 158 January 2011.
'Daughters of Gwerful Mechain' and 'Reading Maps' have been published in *Envoi* issue 154 October 09.
'My Silences', 'Chocolate biscuits' and 'PMT Riddle' have been published in *Obsessed with Pipework* No 48 autumn 2009.
'Stewed Tea' has been published in *Women, identity and religion in Wales,* published by University of Wales press 2018.
'A Parishioner Complains at a Parish Church Council When We Move the Time of Evensong' has been published in *Ink, Sweat and Tears,* January 16th 2022.
'Language Lesson' has been published in *Poetry Wales*, autumn 2010 volume 46 Number 2
'Before the first cremation of the day' has been published in *Poetry Scotland* Issue 103 Spring 2022
'Pen Llŷn' has been published in *Under the Radar* Issue 14 December 2014.

Contents

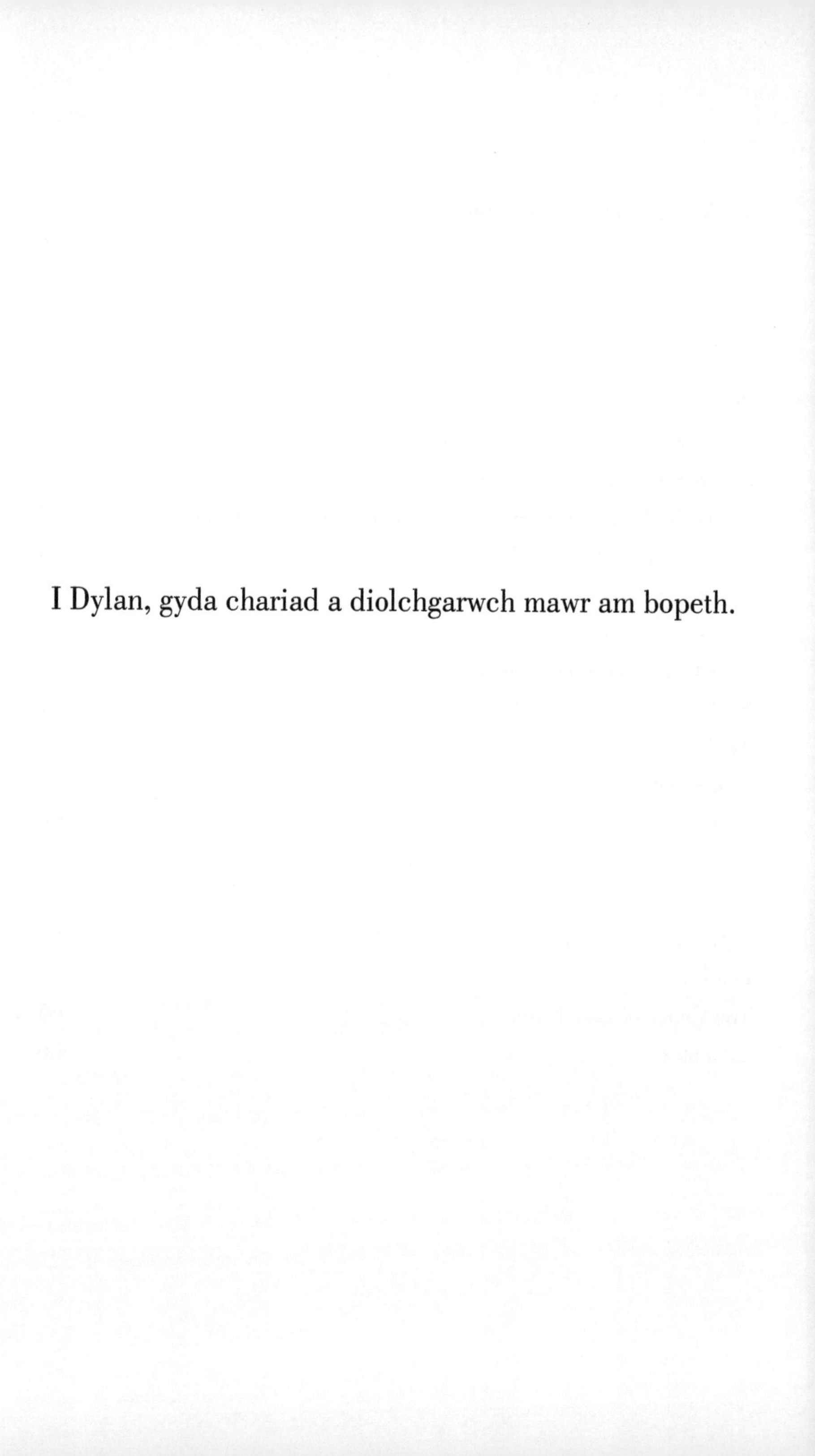

I Dylan, gyda chariad a diolchgarwch mawr am bopeth.

There are only two ways to live your life. One is as though nothing is a miracle. The other is as though everything is a miracle.

attributed to Albert Einstein

Notes from a Eucharistic Life

In Church

Forget the rush
which keeps you
awake.

The heaviness
in your stomach.

Instead

shape your body
into this wood
let its weight
hold you.

Don't look
at the sun's rays
through glass
red, green and blue—

sense the warmth
around your shoulders

let silence
seep in
and around you

look up

and sing.

Another Salem

You walk in late, on your way
to your rightful place
at the margins, or ranked

silenced rows, where you will sit
head bowed in feigned piety
clutching your temple. So say

nothing when your accusers
see devils. Make yourself
small, curse the moment

you were ever centre stage
scrutinised, iconic
selling your soul for soap.

Mother Love

I didn't know you were creating me
garnering what you needed to grow yourself
wounding the sore boundary between us.

If you were just another me
my shame would reject the perfection
of you sleeping—shiny and soothed from your bath
or paddling through summer rivers in Bourton
giddy and larger than Gaia.

My attempts to harness you
are as futile as grappling with existence itself—
death dark rage at ten to nine
fails to deliver two socks
two black shoes a clean red sweatshirt
the library book.

So I can breathe
I hide my detachment in a keepsake box
but you find it.

Now that you have come nothing is safe.

Prodigal

She shambles unnoticed
into the party

calf still swollen
wine still in old wineskins.

The father, who never lets anything get past him
looks up and smiles.

Not much dissolute living there my love
try harder next time...

We'll save the calf till then.

St Peter turns up at a theology conference

He flicks through the information pack
stinking of fish, playing with the keys in his pocket.

He listens intently to instructions of how to get to his room
and where the welcome drinks are held.

He flicks through the timetable.
Do you want to book on to the workshops now?

The woman behind the desk offers:
They get booked up so quickly.

He peers at the titles, he doesn't like to admit
he has no idea what he is reading—

redemption, eucharist, liturgy... Oh and there's one about a Peter
who is an apostle, whatever that is.

He might go along to hear more about this other Peter fellow.
He might find out what apostolic succession and *ekklesia* mean.

He signs up for that and walks away jangling his keys
then turns back and says, *I think I'll stay here for a bit*

do you want some help checking people in?
It will help me feel at home.

Hearth

You have to accept whatever gifts a house gives you—
light through leaves at 9am, a bath that fits you perfectly.

You can spend time and money on soil and seed
but it's the house which gives light, rain and growth.

The way the living room shapes you into rest
as you come home exhausted—this can't be bought.

If the kitchen is a place which will store secrets, truths and dancing
in its cupboards—this cannot be predicted.

A house can't be tried on like a dress
you can't take it back if it doesn't fit.

You have to give yourself to her completely
praying she will give herself to you.

Confession

I was fifty years old
when I learnt that butterflies
can remember being caterpillars.

I wonder if they miss
that rolling in their bodies
as they walked

munching on leaves
and feeling
grounded.

One per cent of caterpillars
are cannibals.
They certainly eat wool.

But change as they say is inevitable.
They must give up on the rolling walk
the feather-like feet.

They must hide in the sticky silence.
They must wait.
They must be patient.

At least that cannibal can now say
that wasn't me. I am beautiful
and look, I can
fly.

Boxes

It's always good to keep the boxes.

So you filled the boiler room
outhouses, back kitchen
big boxes, long boxes
small boxes, strong boxes
polystyrene with its resilient fakery.

It will be handy for when we move.

The house throngs with boxes.
You would have filled our bedrooms
lounge and kitchen... if I had let you.
Open any other door — boxes spill out.

They have pictures of what we bought together.
The cheapest television in the shop.
Non-stick saucepans that stuck.
On others you would write
in deliberate and orderly black—
Computer or *Christmas tree.*

When you left
I kept what I wanted.
You took the things
that mattered most to you.

But you left all the boxes.

PMT Riddle

What surprises me
is not that I get so shouty
and black hearted
but how I manage
to keep so calm
about the things that
really piss me off
for three full weeks
every month.

What I am looking for

is the perfect place to read my book.
An October pub, half a pint of local ale
open fire, sandwiches and chips. An oak table

or a winged chair where I fold myself
staring through the large window at the sea
under a blanket with a large mug of tea.

The book can be theology or a novel
it doesn't even have to be a book.
Maybe I am there with my notebook
writing.

The chair can be any colour
the pub can be in any market town
the chips don't have to be hand cut
it can be whit sun through trees
or dark Michaelmas rain
I am by the fire after all.

I don't care who I'm with
as long as they let me read in peace

because all I am looking for is the perfect place to read my book.

Reading Maps

I'm not sure where we are
she said – he often
let her drive.
He said, *well*
we're good friends
though that would not
have been the question
she dared ask.
She didn't want
to know they were
somewhere
going nowhere.

Stewed Tea

Whenever tea is offered, I take it.
It's bound to be better than the tea
I make. I have it weak, so I make it
too strong. Swirling the bag, again
again. So, no one likes it. They ask
for water instead. But I take their tea.
Always.

Travelling by Train

We sit here swaying, focussed
indifferent. Like secret lovers
keeping friends close, strangers
closer. Stripped bare.
No roles to hide behind. One
sided conversations reveal
who we are, our connections.
The place we don't want to be.

Theology Seminar

She forms her words
like mangoes in her mouth
eyes unconvinced
she has the right to say
‘pedagogy’ ‘womanist’
‘pneumatology’.

Though neither of us
need a dictionary
we still glance
towards the man
in the beard and tie.

They Will Say

First they will say that you shouldn't say those words in your voice
it's too high too squeaky not powerful enough too Welsh.

Then they will say that your shoes make too much noise
or that your earrings are too dangly.

Then they will say that you should light one candle first
but not that one and that your book is on the wrong side.

Then they will say that you can't lead you don't understand detail
or that you focus too much on detail and not enough on the big picture

or that you talk too much or too little
that you are too directive or too passive

that you are too pretty or not pretty enough that you are too thin
or too fat. That you eat too much or don't eat enough.

Then they will say that you feel too much you heard it wrong
that you shouldn't be so sensitive. You're not robust enough.

Then they will say that you are too hard faced.
Don't you care?

Gloria

The Shrine Guardian says she's scruffy
because mud gets everywhere here.

On our retreat, she tells us a story—
one day a couple arrived and asked

where is the shrine guardian? And she said
it's me. She was in her gardening clothes.

They looked her up, and down
and said; *Really?*

The next day setting off for a meeting
I notice Pennant Melangell's mud on my boots.

I leave it there.
Mud needs to get everywhere.

Faith

It's the keeping going when everything has changed.

It's the waking working driving washing
and
doing it all over again the next day.

It's noticing sweet peas
pushing through concrete on Easter day.

It's when my friend reached out
under the airport toilet cubicle
to hold the hand of the woman
who after a long flight
had pissed herself
and was crying.

It's when you see a sunset
through the car window on a long journey home.

It's when you know, however briefly—
you are loved.

In Praise of Opticians

They must always carry mints in their pocket
is my first thought as a woman younger than me
comes close then closer
and my second thought is
I must not forget to breathe.

I see lights everywhere
as she peers into one eye, then the next.
I'm afraid of the machine which blows air into my open eyes
but I'm speaking calmly
joking that I don't like this next bit.
More lights green dots red dots
to my right to my left.
If I have one superpower—it's not showing fear.

So, I'm no longer in this dark room. I think of my Taid
the garage converted into an optical room
with rows and rows of glasses. The room is full of light.
In the mirror, I see me with dark heavy glasses
then me with tortoiseshell rimmed glasses
then me with large teardrop sunglasses
like I saw on *Starsky and Hutch*. I say
I wish I needed glasses.

My Taid says gravely—*don't ever wish that*
as if I had said I wanted cancer or a world war
like the one he served in, leaving Nain behind in Liverpool
having given up nursing
to look after my aunty, and my mother, newly born.
She screamed when she met my Taid for the first time—
he'd been away two years.

Nain is in the kitchen window.
I imagine she has just opened the kitchen drawer full of spectacles
and taken out a pair that were never collected
but help her see her crossword perfectly.
She is smoking, in a blouse, pencil skirt, heels.
In five minutes she will bring in mugs of coffee on a tray.

I'm back in a dark room again. I can see the veins
of my eyes reflected in the light—spindly and red
like rivers on a dark map of Wales.
We go through my family history.
Diabetes, glaucoma, macular degeneration.
She looks at me, then my notes.
I hope it's because I look younger than the numbers on the page say.
It's nothing to worry about she says *it's all age related.*
She is trying to concentrate
on writing up the notes as well as chatting.

I tell her my taid was an optician.
She looks up from her notes.
So was my dad she says.
But I know she doesn't need to hear
about the kitchen drawer full of spectacles, the war or crosswords.

She pauses, smiles and looks away.
I think it was her dad
who told her about the importance
of showing that you're listening—
and of mints.

In Praise of Church Wardens

When she retired, the Church Warden told herself
she would walk to the shop every morning
to pick up her *Daily Post*, so that she talked
to at least one person every day.

But now she goes to church twice a day
to say morning and evening prayer, pick up the linen
and make sure the bookshop money is in the safe
while the Rector's away again with his friend.

He always appreciates the freshly baked loaf
she leaves on his doorstep for his return.
Though he always forgets to leave her a house key.

She'll probably be on her own again in church
for evening prayer, so she will treat herself
and say Compline. It's shorter.
Though it will only be 5 pm.

At least it won't be dark. She misses Harold
and hearing the door creak
his shuffling in from the Home
talking at her about railway timetables and football scores.

She needs to wash the altar cloths
and as she picks up the corporals
she smiles as she remembers the confirmation class
when she explained what the linen was called.

It was nice to be with children again
after being Miss Hubbard for so long.
It's strange that so many people
call her Margaret now

in this new life of hers away from her frail parents
green jars of tadpoles, shells and seaweed
tuneless shouting of 'All Things Bright and Beautiful'
the knock of a ball against a rounders bat.

When she gets home
she picks up a pile of crumpled linen
and irons in the pleats
as if it were a shirt.

In Praise of Hygienists

I'd always wanted to be a priest
my hygienist said, in-between
conversations about her daughter
and my daughter's exam results
after I finally admitted what my job was.

She intones Mesial, Distal and Buccal
and gives me a mark for my oral hygiene.

I make my confession.

In Praise of Burton Services

The last time I was in a service station I was alone
craving peace to read my book.
A man came and sat in the next table though the place was empty.

But I look different now
even if the buzz and white flicker is the same.
One daughter is texting, picking at her five-bean wrap
the other playing with her Nintendo DS.
I snap at her to eat her nuggets.

Rolling news in the distance
—a man has proposed to his girlfriend in court
trying to get her off stabbing him.
She's sent down anyway.

I stare at the shop tempting us with slabs of chocolate
pink and blue cushions only 10.99 for two.
I am enjoying my 5.99 special fish and chips
surprised that the fish is so meaty
the chips fluffy, crispy and hot.
I didn't want mushy peas so I was given sweetcorn instead.
I know we say no exchanges love but it's the end of the day.
You need some feeding up to look after those two lovely girls of yours.

I go to the twin who is still there in hat and pinny
not sure which one cooked for me but I say
That was the best fish and chips I've had in years.
She says with a smile
I cooked it fresh. Nothing worse than chips that have hung around.

I should probably have written this on a form
we know Phil Cooper is the manager for tonight.
She could have got an extra star or even employee of the week
her smiling picture next to Phil's serious babyface.
But this was not the fish of feedback forms.
I refuse to be part of this joyless sterile game.

Will this poem, ten years later, do instead?

In Praise of Alabama 3

The band we've stood for thirty minutes in mud to see
call themselves reverend as nicknames
about to start their divine intervention tour.

Though Rev D Wayne Love has died
and we almost pray to him
in the song 'Hypo Full of Love'.

And I think, if you really want to be a Rev I could teach you
though we both know it is you who has a lot to teach me
about how to live without the brakes on.

I could pull you towards a life of books
assignments and placements
but now you are pulling me back to the music

singing about hoodlums and hoes in your fake American accent
and I imagine you speaking backstage
in your valleys accent, laughing.

Because we are pretending—you are not from Alabama
there are more than three of you
and I am in on the joke

because you said you are here for the losers and the misfits
even me in my daisy top, long denim shorts
and I've never taken drugs in my life.

You don't sing my favourite song 'Peace in the Valley'
that song you dedicated to Gary Speed
in the concert in Wrexham, the week he died,

breaking the fake accent, admitting you are Welsh.
I now think of him when I listen to it
and all the desperate people I have buried
who had no way out and their funeral songs.

The only funeral song I didn't know was by 50 cent.
All the rest I say, *ah yes, good choice*
and families look at me open mouthed

because a Vicar listens to the same music
as broken families do, and desperate people do.
My playlist is full of funeral processionals and recessionals.

In *Hello I'm Johnny Cash* the guitarist walks up smiling
he knows this will get a laugh as the words are sung
Were you there when they crucified the Lord.

He stands as a cross, backing singers fake praying
the harmonica player placing sellotape
as if it's a halo above his head.

But I'm not offended. The day when music
doesn't get angry with God or mock him
is when we know the Church is really dead.

At the end of the set we go and find
some burgers and chips.
The drum beating in my chest.

Daughters of Gwerful Mechain

Isn't everyone's relationship with God like that?
I wanted to ask, while our teacher
told us Ann Griffiths was a mystic.
At seventeen, boys are all-consuming
even God. Now she lines the cold path
to Llanfihangel Church. Blue Books

betrayed her legacy, leaving us heavy
gold edged Bibles, green gloss paint
strict metre four part harmonies
(unless your tenor has died
or your alto's babysitting grandchildren).
Our rooms—front parlours sagging

with respectability. Ceramic angels
genteel ladies, china cups gleaming
like women's sacrificed souls
on Wales' mantelpiece altar.
Ann, join with us and all
the daughters of Gwerful Mechain.

Let us dig up her work, plunder
our birth right, cast off
Victoriana felt and brass that stops us
breathe. Hunger for a passionate
God. Adore our bodies.
Relish the world.

A Parishioner Complains at a Parish Church Council When We Move the Time of Evensong

You have changed the Bible you have changed the words in the service you have brought in girls to serve at the altar and women can now be sidesmen and any minute now you will let that priestess next door with her earrings and clacky heels come and take the service when you're on holiday and anyone can now read the lessons but I liked it better when it was just me and the headmaster and we now pray for all people instead of all men and you have changed the creed to say that it was for us and our salvation that Jesus came and not for us men and you have changed the words of Onward Christian Soldiers where would you be without our soldiers we would be speaking in German and you want to charge a pound for coffee a pound this isn't Starbucks we've always had coffee in the coffee morning for 50p and it was nicer it was made with milk not water and now you are moving the time of evensong from six to six thirty this really really really takes the biscuit.

Resistance

When we watched the five nations
my dad would be in his winged chair.
I would be on the sofa reading.
My mam would kneel in front of the TV
willing JJ and JPR on as they ran towards the touchline.

There is nothing in the world as free as Gerald
in our own 22, dodging the Scots
throwing to Bennett, on to Burcher
and then Burcher lobbing the ball to Fenwick
Fenwick to Bennett with an astonishing pass
and Bennett sidestepping one, then two Scottish players
and looking up, sees an open field and runs and runs.
It's a try!

But the English when they marched towards our boys
seemed invincible. When they grabbed the ball
and ran, my mam would shout *stopiwch nhw!*
As if her weak cry could make a difference.

As if she is at the battle of Dyrham in 577
with a leek on her helmet, facing the Anglo Saxons.
Or in Chester in 1277 watching with dread
as Edward starts his invasions or in 1301
in Caernarfon as he is crowning his baby son as Prince of Wales
joking that he can't speak a word of English.
As if she is pleading with education inspectors
not to write their hateful comments
about us being uncivilized and immoral into blue books
or is protesting in 1965 as Capel Celyn
is flooded to provide water for Liverpool.

She is now in 1282 at Cilmeri
whispering to Llewelyn *this is a trap!*

Even now, watching the six nations
she never gives up hope that her *stopiwch nhw*
will summon Owain Glyndŵr himself from his hiding place
to run onto the field in red, tearing off
the *Ich dien* feathers in disgust
cradling our dignity in his arm.

Running with Vicky Feaver

So I have arrived at St Andrews for a poetry festival
as I'm a rookie I let Kim choose our itinerary.

I am late and she is late and we don't know where
we are going. This is how we became friends.

She arrived late for the course at Tŷ Newydd
not being able to read a map and I thought

this is also me. We are in front of Toppings book shop
not yet inside drinking coffee and eating a brownie

browsing poetry. That will come later.
No, at the moment we are late.

We need to find Parliament Hall –
we see an older woman, she looks like a poetry fan

so we ask *Do you know where Parliament Hall is?*
Yes she said *that's where I'm going, follow me.*

So we are running through St Andrews following Vicky Feaver
though we didn't know she was Vicky Feaver then.

She could have said, *I am Vicky Feaver*
not a shepherd for lost poetry fans.

We are running like they run in films. Dodging
cars and pedestrians. Running as if nothing matters

but arriving at Parliament Hall. We're here just in time.
We clamber over serious looking people

to find folding chairs, we prize them open
as quietly as we can. Vicky Feaver has gone

to sit with her friend and we smile an awkward goodbye
perching gingerly on squeaky chairs.

We flick through the programme and see her picture
alongside one of the events. The woman

we've just been running with is Vicky Feaver!
When I grow up to be a poet I want to be Vicky Feaver.

She is a poet, but she can still read maps.
She has a great name. She knows where she is going.

She is happy to be in front of an audience.
Happy to be ordinary. It's all the same to her.

She just loves the poetry.
And helping people.

Five Wise Virgins

It's not that I am a planner exactly
it's just that I've learnt
from my many and various mistakes.

That time when I forgot
to switch off my straighteners
and it was hot three days later.

Or when I nearly ran out of petrol
begging the lad minding the shop
who wanted to get away to play snooker

telling him I would be stuck on the Berwyns
late at night with no phone signal
if he didn't serve me.

One weekend away I forgot my suitcase
and I made do with what I had
in my handbag emergency kit.

Those virgins weren't wise
because they were planners
but because they were learners.

Samaritan

You're so far away from home.
You have no idea how you got here.

You sit in the road, dazed
wondering why all these religious people
are passing you by.

But you know it's not about them—
it's about waiting for the right one.

To allow yourself to be loved.

The Tax Collector and the Sinner

If prayer changes us
how is it that those who claim
to pray the longest
stay the same?

Do they spend that time
imagining God
with thumbs up, whispering:
Well done, keep doing
what you're doing,
You're great!

Language Lesson

Manon...claims she heard no echoes, never sang in her own language.
Christine Evans, Second Language

You made us touch wet wood, called it
flotsam. Though we could smell
launderette steam, and school was still
there, behind the Council's wall of flats.

This beach, where Jones Biol. clamped
a found embryo in a jar, and cold girls
skulked during Games. *Crush seaweed,*
stroke stone, you said. *You are writers now.*

One teacher told us, *Mae'r iaith yn bwysig*
ond dydw i ddim yn Welsh Nash
whilst you were leading us towards
a space of our own, between language

and *iaith*. I found a new voice shaped
by shells, buzzard skulls, and always
the sea. Now I scold my daughters
—*Siaradwch yn Gymraeg!*

but Miriam claims her school
has an English Not.
Yet, like mother's guilt, *mamiaith*
grows, and pulls, draws back, rushes in.

My Silences

The silence that is frustration.
I am voiceless because I can't say that.
You would be shocked, disturbed.

The silence from not belonging.
I don't want to say something stupid.
I am not good enough to be here.

The silence when words falter.
I am only learning to speak, but I have to be
confident and strong before you will listen.

The silence because no one has said this before.
I don't want to be the first...
but I'll join in with you if you say it.

The silence from having two languages
and the word has fallen through the gap.

The silence because I have so much to say—
where do I begin?

The silence because you have stopped talking
and I have stopped listening.

The silence because I am full.
I feel peace. I am satisfied.
There's no need to say anything
because you understand.

The silence that comes from not speaking—
because there's no other living being.
I can't hear anything but the sound of my breathing
and occasionally my singing.

Hiraeth riddle

As I grew up I was told that we had a word
which no one else had.
A word meaning nostalgia.
A word about sadness and loss.

I remember a poem I learnt off by heart at school
about *hiraeth* being in the sea
the mountains
in silence and in song.

But nearly every language
has a word that means *hiraeth.*

At a poetry festival, a Portuguese American got up
and told us about *saudade*
a constant feeling of absence
the sadness of something that's missing.
He told us that this word is untranslatable.

But this word is *sehnsucht* in German, *dor* in Romanian
tizita in Ethiopian, *assouf* in the language of the Tuareg
clivota in Slovak. In Czech it is *stesk.*
in Turkish—*hazret*
in America the language of the blues.

Every language apart from one
has an untranslatable word
that means *hiraeth.*
A word about sadness and loss.

Gospel

I didn't want to know about bed bugs I thought to myself
as I watched *Pebble Mill at One*, home from school with a cold.

I could have done without seeing their monstrous images
enlarged in black and white. Because facts are best ignored.

That day I found out something that transformed my life.

How to change a double duvet. Each time I wash my sheets
(admittedly not enough) I always give thanks for her.

That red-haired woman and her advice.
It's so genius I want to tell everyone about it. In fact—

I am now outside your door in my suit, scrubbed child in tow
though no leaflet in my hand, just a duvet cover.

When you open the door, you sigh when you see me.
I ask *Have you heard the good news?* You stare.

I ask *Do you know how to change a duvet cover?*
And before you open your mouth I say—

You turn the cover inside out. Then you put your arms all the way in
and grab both corners. You then grab the corners of the duvet.

There's no hard work for you, no pulling or pushing or fiddling
because it sorts itself out. All you have to do is to shake it.

And then you shake it.

And you shake it.

Prayer

Pray for me if you like he said
hardened raw by old pain
It won't make a difference.

Though the universe shifts in discomfort.
In the dark a poem emerges
bloody and wet from another world
screaming a truth.

In a sunlit classroom,
pupils and teacher share a silence.

In an airless boardroom
a catholic and a protestant laugh at a joke.

A crocus unfolds.
A sparrow trills.

The day I started asking questions

We arrived laughing, stepping through snow
the nuns at the centre were delighted to see us, thrilled
that women could be priests at last in their sister church.

We brought champagne and chocolate left over from Christmas.
In our talks the Archdeacon told us what the old, old words meant.
Words women could now say. Jesus' words around a table.

Sometimes the Archdeacon used long English, Greek and Latin words
and he spoke about change—that we would be different now.
That the Church would be different now.

And all long they didn't know that I was eight weeks pregnant.

Terrified I would also lose this baby.
Ashamed I might bleed in the service.
Glad that I was sick every afternoon.

In our last talk he said *ossified*. I started then paused
What does ossified mean?
The women laughed. The Archdeacon coloured.

I am stupid. I say such long words don't I.
It means becoming hardened
like a bone.

In our last service we heard from Isaiah's prophecy.
See I am doing a new thing.
Do you not perceive it?

After the laying on of hands, during the applause
Kathy and I sobbed and laughed
turned away from the cameras and held each other.

Afterwards, when nearly everyone had gone
the Bishop who had laid his hands on my head
now laid them on my stomach.

Consecration in the time of Covid

In Chichester, two bishops will be consecrated
one is a woman, the other is a man.

The man does not think that women
should be ordained
but will work happily with the woman.
The woman will pretend
she accepts that the man
does not think she should be there
and that she doesn't feel ashamed.

Because of the virus, this will be live-streamed.
Those present will be tested to see if they carry it.
They will wear masks to make sure they don't leak it
or that it's not leaked onto them.
They will need to wash their hands for twenty seconds.
They will need to disinfect their hands with sanitisers.
There will not be any touching and definitely no hugging.

The Archbishop of Canterbury
will 'graciously restrain' himself from ordaining
because once he has touched the woman
he cannot touch the man.
But he will hand them both a pastoral staff
with a disinfected hand.

Disinfected of Covid I mean
not of woman.

While the Church was meeting to vote on Women Bishops

I spoke to a local politician canvassing on my doorstep
led an assembly for ninety-five children on the Walls of Jericho
finalised arrangements for a Diocesan Theology Course
started a sermon on the woman and the lost coin
cooked spaghetti Bolognese for my family
prepared a couple for their child's baptism
wrote some more words on research methodology for a PhD
spoke on the phone to someone who'd had bad news
went shopping in Llandudno to buy new winter boots
put clothes in the washing machine then the dryer
did the washing up again and again
cooked chicken biryani for my family
watched *Cinema Paradiso* and cried
wrote 57 emails
started to think about a Macmillan coffee morning
met with the parish leadership team
to plan which services to have for Harvest and Christmas
to discuss objections to our ideas about reordering the building
to plan our celebration for the graveyard which has received another award

and did the washing up again
and wrote another 23 emails.

The Train from Holyhead

Do not neglect to show hospitality to strangers
for thereby some have entertained angels unawares.

Hebrews 13:2

I catch the train in Colwyn Bay.
A man is talking loudly on his phone
to a silent secretary. It's not good enough
that the meeting has been double booked.
A couple are carefully unwrapping foil-
wrapped sandwiches and homemade cakes.
They open flasks, pour out dribbles of tea
into tiny flask tops.

A man in his thirties
tattoos on his right hand and both arms
is drinking beer
a dog in tow.
Where is he going?
Where has he come from?
He likes to talk. His accent fluctuates.
Irish? Brummie? Geordie? We don't know.

He has stood outside 'Marksies'
in Llandudno selling *The Big Issue.*
He has been at the Vicar's door
asking for train money.
He has sat cross-legged outside Greggs
smiling at the passers-by.
Now he's here, with his questions.
His truth telling. I avoid his gaze.

Advent

I was in prison
and you said that my cell was like a hotel
you didn't want it in your town
you didn't want to pay for it.

I was homeless
and you said that I couldn't sleep here.
If you used our church as a night shelter
we would have to roll up the carpet
it might get frayed
and we have just paid for it.
And would you want to use our toilet?

I was an alcoholic
and you didn't want my support group to meet in your hall.
You said you didn't want to encourage
that sort of person to come in here.

I was sick
and you said you didn't want to form a visiting team
to offer pastoral care –
you felt that it was you who needed support.

I was poor
and you said that God helps those
who help themselves.

I was a child
and you told me to be quiet
and to sit still
and not to ask questions.

I was hungry
and you said, here, you can have this tin
for your foodbank.
It's out of date anyway.

Chocolate biscuits

I stare at bourbons, pink wafers
custard creams, yet this time
he is not laughing at my work

and tying my words in knots.
I am not wondering what the script
he has written will sound like this time.

No more fear that my heartbeat
is thudding around echoing
barren rooms. It's over.

I unwrap a big, round chocolate biscuit
and eat it. Melted brown-ness sticks
to my fingers. I lick it off. I am a child.

I want to eat all the biscuits
smear chocolate all over the walls
as a sickly dirty protest. Instead

I smooth silver foil with my thumbs
fold it, over and over again into a tiny square
shining tightly like newborn skin.

I put it in my pocket.
When I walk out of the room
I will write my own dialogue

and in my new life I shall do
what the hell I like.
And not just with chocolate biscuits.

Transfiguration August 6th 1995

i.m. Sophie Hook

even the darkness is not dark to you
the night is as bright as the day
for darkness is as light to you.
Psalm 139

So I stood in the pulpit, a young girl myself
some would say. The Rector was away.
I was left to grasp at words in the air

to articulate our despair, trying to make sense
of the murder of a child in our town.
It was Transfiguration Day.

In our reading, we hear of a mountain top
Jesus burning in white light
before his long journey.

On that Sunday I didn't speak of love.
I may have mentioned hope, but even then
I shouldn't have. We wouldn't have been ready.

This Transfiguration Day we can only speak of horror.
We know the journey we must take.

Mother Church is a Feeder

The cakes in the tin waiting for visitors to call
the sausage rolls, egg sandwiches in triangles, bara brith
to welcome the new priest or for the funeral tea—
it's all the same.

Jesus invited us to his supper
but he didn't mean Welsh cakes, scones with jam and cream
on doilies with Battenberg and Tunnocks tea cakes.

They called him a glutton and a drunkard.
Ah go on, just another slice of chocolate cake.
Don't be silly, you're so slim.
It should be me who should be losing weight!

So we make these generous cooks and bakers kneel.
Tell them to open wide.
Stick a thin wafer on their tongues and
slam their mouths shut.

Apple

I'm in a nursing home seeing Margaret's sister.
I'm bringing out a silver box
with a wafer, a candle, a prayer book
and I say
In the name of God…

I hadn't been sure which language she had wanted.
In Llandudno her generation spoke Welsh at home
but those words are long gone now
though she likes her room to be like *a pin in paper*
and asks *could I keep the chair* after I leave
and sighs, *old age, it doesn't come by itself you know.*

These words we are saying are neither English nor Welsh
for her, but another
Spirit, trespass, bread.
We say a prayer together and she says
We do not presume
to come to this your table, merciful Lord
trusting in our own righteousness
but in your manifold and great mercies.
We are not worthy
so much as to gather up the
crumble
under your table.

And I am at home in Nefyn
the smell of apples baking in the kitchen
and Jesus is there with my mother
gin and tonic in hand
hitching up his white robe
hoovering the floor.

A priest at the altar rail 1

They open their hands
as if they have nothing to give.
They open their mouths
as if they have nothing to say.
They walk away filled.
I remain here empty.

A priest at the altar rail 2

They kneel here with open hands.

Rough hands
that milked cows this morning.

The wild garlic hands
of the gardener.

Hands of the retired civil servant
with stray hairs on his palms.

The plump hands of the widow
who comes here once a week to touch.

Hands of the engineer
who designed systems at the MOD.

The pink hands of the woman
who looks silent and submissive here
but who slaps and jabs me
if I change the hymns.

Hands that for twenty years
handled cash at the garage
while all her friends left.

The hands of the man
who refuses to shake my hand
because I am a woman priest.

Hands that held rifles
teaching young men to shoot.

Hands that make jam for the coffee morning
and the annual harvest bread.

Hands
hands open
hands expecting something.

Before the first cremation of the day

No undertaker barking at colleagues in black to lift the coffin.
No supervisor quipping into the pretty curate's ear.
No clergy in the vestry gossiping committees and promotions.
No murmuring by the congregation shivering outside the door.
No nursing home manager expressing condolences in serious tones.
No mother hissing at her adult children to put the smokes away.

That will come later.

Now there is only the sound of car tyres on gravel.
Whispers from the office discussing the order of the day.
Ovens firing up. Seagulls squawking.
Shouts from the scrapyard next door.

Natals not mortals

This year I bought gerbera.
I learnt that they attract bees, butterflies and birds
but are resistant to deer. We have no deer.
I watered them every day
and they flowered and flowered.
In mid-August the leaves withered
the brown petals dropped off.
I grabbed at the stems
about to throw them away
when Dylan said—*why not just dead head them?*
As I snipped off the heads, I noticed tiny buds
like children closing their eyes so tight
pretending to be asleep.
And I imagined the gerbera in the gardening bin
the men with their shouts and gloves
sliding the bin on to their machine
and the gerbera there in the mulch
tightly closing their eyes
knowing that soon they can open their eyes
and bloom and bloom and bloom.

A priest at a funeral

I need all the rage I can muster
to keep this calm; to sculpt space
to hold shifting, fragile colours.

I marvel at how midwives day by day
caress women into their own artistry
weaving love like expectant shawls.

I am the last to stroke the wood
that bears this ending; gathering
enough fragments of courage

to let it fall through my fingers
chanting hope, forgiveness, dust.

Pen Llŷn

We cling to our corner, always aware
we live on an edge. No-one on earth
like us with our shifting white
and silver light on slate, gorse and fern.

And the sea, with its song, its danger.

We try to leave, though we know
nothing matters but creating
soil and returning dust.

The House of Lost Things

My daughters tell me *Mam, you're always good at finding things*
because I would always find what was lost, where it was meant to be.

I would ask *where did you last see it?* and I would find it
fallen under the table, or behind a pile of books.

When they called, I would warn them
I hope I'm not going to find it straight away!

What they don't know is that I always have lost things in my life.
I haven't seen my purple bracelet for years and my new jade top

has been missing for a month. I am even writing this poem
on an envelope because I have lost my poetry book.

When she was eighteen, my daughter admitted she would hide
her shoes, when she was five, so that she was late for school

and I would be standing there in the hall, hot and white.
Now my other daughter is tidying her room before she goes away.

After years of war against books, toys and clothes
each stack is being catalogued, recycled or put in the attic

as if she is already leaving in her own mind and mine.
As if half of her is already a ghost. In her room

I talk of a new study, but I promise to keep the red wall.
I imagine myself in a month wandering around this house of lost things

peering into cupboards and wardrobes, looking behind clothes
and under bedside tables, trying to find the time

I had always claimed to strangers was going too fast
the time that is always here, in this moment.

Endnotes

Another Salem

Vosper's Salem, a painting of Sian Tŷ'n y Fawnog in her traditional Welsh dress walking into chapel was bought by Lord Leverhulme in 1909 and became ubiquitous in Wales when prints were given away for vouchers from Lever Brothers' Sunlight Soap. There is a tradition that the devil can be seen in the folds of the shawl, revealing her 'pride'.

Resistance

stopiwch nhw! is stop them!

Daughters of Gwerful Mechain

Ann Griffiths was an 18th C Welsh hymn writer, and Gwerful Mechain a 15th C female Welsh poet who wrote on themes of embodied sexuality as well as about religion and faith.

The Blue Books refers to the report from the 1847 Inquiry into the State of Education in Wales, which was heavily critical of the morality of Welsh women, resulting in the churches imposing strict moral codes.

Language Lesson

This poem was written in response to Christine Evans' poem about my English class, and several of my classmates, including myself, are mentioned.

The translations are:

Mae'r iaith yn bwysig ond dydw i ddim yn Welsh Nash
language is important but I'm not a Welsh Nationalist

Iaith—language

Siaradwch yn Gymraeg!—Speak in Welsh!

Mamiaith—mother tongue

The Welsh Not was given to Welsh schoolchildren to punish and stigmatise them for speaking Welsh in school. More commonly it was a wooden plaque with WN inscribed on it. It was passed from child to child when they were caught speaking in Welsh and whoever was wearing or holding it at the end of the day was beaten (18-20th C).

Apple

In the second stanza, the italics denote literal translations of Welsh idioms, phrases which Welsh monoglot English speakers say in Wales, not realising they are originally Welsh idioms.

www.ingramcontent.com/pod-product-compliance
Ingram Content Group UK Ltd.
Pitfield, Milton Keynes, MK11 3LW, UK
UKHW031928270726
14063UKWH00001B/68